KINDLE

UNLIMITED

7 Tips to Maximizing Kindle
Unlimited Subscription Account
Benefits and Getting the Most from
Your Kindle Unlimited Books

By JOSHUA ELANS

Table of Contents

Introduction 3

Chapter 1: What is the Kindle Unlimited Subscription? 5

Chapter 2: Questions About the Kindle Unlimited Subscription
....7

Chapter 3: Pros and Cons of the Kindle Unlimited
Subscription 11

Chapter4: Comparing Kindle Unlimited to Other EBook
Services 15

Chapter 5: Interesting Features...17

Chapter6: How is it different from the Kindle lending library?
....20

Chapter7: *Signing Up* 23

Conclusion...28

Introduction

Upon its launch in 2007, Kindle was a novelty product. It enjoyed instant popularity. The Kindle allows you to carry an entire library's worth of reading material wherever you may go. Affordable and easy to use, it gives avid readers the joy of accessing millions of authors and titles. Many other versions of the kindle have been released since its initial release. Newer kindles have updated features, such as touchscreen and mobile phone technology.

With a Wi-Fi connection, the kindle enables you to download books and store them on your device. Lightweight and easy to transport, it is now a regular on vacations, coffee houses and long legs of travel. Kindles are also amazing for the storage of documents; you can have them right on your device. They are also extremely easy to manage; the instructions are very clear and precise. The capability to read any book at any time, in practically any setting, is another reason kindles have become so loved. High-tech, but easy to manage, the Amazon kindle gives you your library at you fingertips.

How can you make the most of the new and exciting options the kindle unlimited has to offer? How can I manage my unlimited subscription to get the most benefits? What little "secrets" are there to maximizing my abilities to navigate and use my unlimited subscription? How I can cancel my kindle unlimited subscription? In this great book, you will discover kindle tips in a way you never imagined. You will become a kindle maven, exploring the secrets of your unlimited subscription and exploiting every benefit.

Chapter 1: What is the Kindle Unlimited Subscription?

The kindle unlimited subscription allows you to have access to thousands of books and audiobooks, for a small monthly fee. The concept of having reading materials so easy and quick is what the kindle is all about. There are thousands of authors to choose from. You can choose the eBook or the audio version of that book. You can read anything out of the collection of approximately 700,000 books and listen to approximately 200,000 audio books. Think of it as a library, but without the due dates. With many best sellers on the list available, you can pick and choose as many books a month as you want. You have unlimited reading and unlimited listening.

You can, however only download a certain number of books monthly, but it makes little difference, as once the books are downloaded, they stay on your device as long as your subscription remains active. That is unless you reach the ten book limit in the same month, then you will need to choose one book to return. There are thousands of kindle exclusives on the list you choose from, and these books are only found on kindle!

You can choose from the long novel type of reading, to quick one hundred paged books for more light reading. Along with all these amazing books, you also enjoy all the fantastic kindle features you have come to love. The other beneficial part of the kindle unlimited subscription is that you can use it on practically any device, from android phones to iPad.

Again think of it as a library, where you won't be the owner of the book, but you don't have a due date until you pass the ten book limit. Then you will have to choose what book you want to return. Even upon returning the book, everything that you did to the book, such as notes and comments, will reappear every time you have the book on your device.

To get all the benefits of a Kindle unlimited subscription, all you need to do is go into your account and sign up for the service. You will be given a thirty-day free trail. This gives you the opportunity to use and understand the workings of the service, before committing to monthly payments. Most avid readers find that their unlimited subscription is extremely suitable for their reading needs and enjoyment. The long list of authors and book titles available can seem overwhelming at first, but you will quickly be able to find what you are looking for. It's basically the "Netflix" of the literary world.

Chapter 2: Questions About the Kindle Unlimited Subscription

Now that you have a basic idea about what kindle unlimited subscription is, there are most likely questions that arise. In this chapter, we will cover some of the most frequently asked questions in reference to the kindle unlimited subscription.

1. *How many titles are currently available on kindle unlimited?*

There are currently over one million titles available for kindle unlimited. There is a fantastic variety of interesting books to enjoy. Kindle unlimited currently is loaded with titles that are exclusive only to kindle. You won't find them in any other eBook service.

2. *Are there many big, bestsellers on kindle unlimited?*

Since many major publishing houses shied away from associating with kindle unlimited, you won't actually find many of the "big" authors available. What you will find, however, is a whole new world of authors to explore. You will also find no longer in print classics. All this variety opens up an entire universe of book diversity.

3. *Is kindle unlimited an affordable option?*

Yes, it is. Most people invest in an unlimited subscription for the affordability. This is especially true if you read more than three books a month. The books are also low priced if you are keen on the chosen title becoming part of your permanent library.

4. *Is finding eBooks that are available to me on kindle unlimited easy?*

Actually, yes, from the main unlimited page to the flagged books, finding eBooks that are compatible to your unlimited subscription is quite easy.

Flagged books? That simply means that on the list of _all_ kindle titles, there is a little flag next to the book cover that indicates its obtainability on kindle unlimited.

5. How does my unlimited subscription include audiobooks?

The kindle unlimited subscription audiobooks are basically every book that you put on your device and you can switch it from reading to audio. By selecting the "with narration" icon, you can hear what you were reading.

When you sign on for the free thirty-day trial unlimited subscription, it includes a three-month subscription to audiobooks. With that, you will obtain audio credits, one per month; you then use that to listen to your selected audiobook.

6. Do I get to keep all my books, if I cancel my unlimited subscription?

No, once you cancel your subscription, all the books in your unlimited library will also be absent. If you decide to later reactivate your unlimited subscription, then your books will return, along with any notes, bookmarks and highlights you made to that particular reading material.

7. Do I have to buy a kindle to have admittance to kindle unlimited subscription?

No, you do not. The great advantage to kindle's unlimited subscription is that it is companionable with any device.

Any other questions you may have can be answered on the Amazon website or directly on the kindle unlimited subscription page.

Chapter 3: Pros and Cons of the Kindle Unlimited Subscription

What are some of the pros and cons of the kindle unlimited subscription?

As with everything you involve yourself in, there is the good side, and not so good side. Here we will go over some of these, by comparing and contrasting them to help you reach a fair conclusion about the practicality of your Kindle unlimited subscription.

Pros

One of the first, probably the most important pro of the kindle unlimited subscription is the availability of literature. Having a higher selection of books gives the opportunity to choose from many titles, as well as many genres. The wide selection of authors also helps you to discover new styles of writing you may have not noticed before. It really draws you in and supports you to discern interesting books that may have not ever been on your regular reading lists. The infinite choice just gives you a whole new perspective on reading.

The affordability of the kindle unlimited subscription is also extremely appealing. Monthly, it costs less than a coffee and donut, and has better benefits as well. The ease at which you can subscribe and unsubscribe, make it a wise choice for those whom may feel intimidated by managing other kinds of subscriptions.

When you pick a book to put on your device through kindle unlimited subscription you are supporting fresh authors. Self-published authors usually have trouble breaking into the literary field, due to the large publishing corporations. Kindle unlimited subscription supports and subsidizes many new authors. Kindle unlimited subscription also helps authors to promote their newest work, by giving subscribers deals on said books.

The books that you find on kindle's unlimited subscription list have passed rigorous quality control testing. This means that both the reader and the author can rest easy that they are receiving and being accredited for a high-quality product.

You can use your kindle unlimited subscription on many different devices.

That can be useful during long trips, where your device may be out of reach.

Audiobooks are only to be found on kindle unlimited subscription, at this affordable price. The easiness with which the subscriber can switch between reading and listening to the book is incomparable.

All these fantastic pros are wonderful reasons to invest in the kindle unlimited subscription. They really do pay for themselves and give you such a wide selection of reading materials. You'll never be without!

Cons

The five biggest, traditional publishing houses are not associated with Kindle unlimited subscriptions. You may not find an author you are looking for due to that fact. But, the wide selection guarantees that you will find many that you do enjoy.

The ten books a month limit can seem strict in comparison with other eBook subscriptions. Where this differs from others is that you can keep eBooks on your device, as long as the subscription remains active, and then trade them when you see fit, as long as you maintain the ten book limit. With many others, you have a "due date" and must return the book at that date.

The availability of such a wide range of choices may confuse you at first, but once you understand how to use your kindle unlimited subscription, it's a piece of cake.

As a reader, you there is not a feature to allow you to preview the book using "excerpts". There is a brief summary of what the book is about, but not actually from the books contents.

There are pros and cons to everything. They help us in making the right decisions when we weigh them out and process them.

Chapter4: Comparing Kindle Unlimited to Other EBook Services

EBook services have become a lasting detail in the literary world. Since they are all offering essentially the same service, each has to do their best to provide unique attributes. There is a lot of competition and kindle unlimited subscriptions definitely have their work cut out for them.

The pricing of the other major competitors is almost the same, give or take a dollar. They are all monthly subscriptions, which gives you the tractability to budget. All give you a free thirty-day trial, so that you can fully explore the benefits of your monthly subscription. Kindle unlimited is the only monthly subscription that works with any device. The others need specific devices for compatibility reasons. Kindle unlimited also offers audiobooks, whereas others may not make available that option. With all eBook amenities, you have unrestricted admittance to the entire library. You may enjoy as many books as you want, for as long as you want, with no due dates.

Unlike other eBook services, kindle unlimited subscription is not an application, but an actual subscription that you sign up with through Amazon. The unlimited book listings is a combination of free and pay for titles, and you have the right to use to them all. You can later buy the pay for books, if you want them on your device, as a part of your collection. Kindle unlimited subscription is best if you want more popular, modern series and titles.

The other eBook services are through applications, which may not be well-suited to all your devices like the kindle unlimited subscription is.

These subscriptions often have many of the similar titles, but there are many that are exclusive to kindle unlimited subscription. That makes it a unique platform to enrich your literary familiarity. An eBook subscription service is a great way to pick up and read individual titles, which you may have passed by otherwise. Kindle unlimited subscription is one of the better subscription services available, in that it allows you to use it with any device, including cell phones. This convenience makes it one of the most valuable services. The comfort of audiobooks also makes it one of the most attractive subscription services currently on the market.

Chapter 5: Interesting Features

The kindle unlimited subscription has many interesting features. These features make it easy to choose and select your personal monthly library. Kindle unlimited is often referred to as the "Netflix" of the literary world. It has over 640,000 titles to choose from. There are many modern titles, as well as beloved classics. What needs to be very clear is that you don't "buy" the books you download while using your unlimited subscription. You are effectively borrowing them.

The great advantage that gives you is along with your regular kindle library, you now have a lending library, which can consistently be refreshed and renewed. This is great when you discover a new author or genres, but aren't ready to completely commit to buying the whole series. Kindle unlimited is fantastic for shopping around to broaden your literary interests. Many books that are no longer in print are available for your enjoyment. We all have that one classic we've always wanted to read, but never go around to it. This subscription provides you with the ability to make that goal tangible.

Searching for books in kindle unlimited is very simple. It is the same as looking for any book on kindle, plus they have their own list that allows easy access. Access Kindle unlimited page from Amazon.com. On this page, there will appear highlighted and highly recommendable books. You can also use the entire kindle unlimited book listing. Narrow down what you are looking for by putting in the author's name, book title, or keywords. The search feature helps you to better find what you are looking for. Also, on the Amazon site, where books are listed, many of them have a small tag on top of the books letting you know that they are included in the unlimited subscription.

There is a comprehensive list of ideal titles that are included in the kindle unlimited subscription. You can re-read old favorites. The Lord of the Rings is always a great read. The complete Harry Potter series is available through kindle unlimited. You can relive these fascinating stories, and anywhere you would like. No carrying around bulky books on that long flight.

Learning new skills is another upside of the kindle unlimited subscription. You can begin perfecting a skill in no time. There is an extensive selection of "how to" titles, as well as do it yourself. There are countless hobby books and cookbooks as well. With the ever changing monthly library, you can cook new and tasty new meals daily. Build a bird house or create your own cosmetics. These books are interesting, and once you have perfected the new skill, you return the book and start with a new one. The learning of new skill is great because it often piques curiosity about similar skill sets.

If you get tired of reading and are really into your book, you can use the Audible, that comes with your kindle unlimited subscription. This audible feature is great also for long road trips. It's also great for kids because they can be easily amused while learning. Storytelling is a dying art, but kindle revives it with this unique feature. Keeping the children occupied while you safely drive cross country to Grams is a huge plus. Also, hearing a story expands the imagination. It is just as useful to you if you travel a lot for work or find yourself in traffic. What better than a lovely story to make the morning commute seem shorter?

Browsing for your next literary adventure is appealing. You may find books that you might not have ever discovered otherwise. Kindle unlimited also is a great place to find up and coming authors. You can come across many self-published books, helping support the smaller author community. You never know what new writer will catch your fancy. All this pleasurable reading for a monthly low price, unlimited escapades, and encounters!

Chapter6: How is it different from the Kindle lending library?

Kindle offers many great services with all its products. It has quickly become a constant feature in the enthusiastic reader's inventory. Kindle's unlimited subscription is another one of those great advantages of having a connection with the Kindle products. As mentioned earlier, kindle unlimited subscription is based on a fixed fee, where you have the choice to borrow up to ten books monthly. Sounds a lot like a library, right? Then, as a consumer of kindle products, you're well aware of kindle's lending library. You may ask yourself, what is the difference?

Firstly, the two services are subscription based, so that may cause some confusion with buyers. Secondly, they both allow you to enjoy your books without having to buy individual titles. These things are stunningly similar, but both services are worlds apart from one another. It's also worth mentioning that they are not competing with one another, each has its set of compensations to provide an easy, comfortable service to clientele.

The lending library includes other forms of entertainment, movies, and music. The unlimited subscription is books and audiobooks.

The monthly cost varies as well. Kindle unlimited has a price of $9.99 monthly, where the lending library is a bit less, at $8.25 a month. Why the difference in pricing? The difference in pricing is due to each subscription program's different rewards. In the lending library, you can have one book at a time to keep on your device monthly, whereas in the unlimited subscription you can keep ten titles on your device, monthly. With the lending library, even if you finish a book and return it, you are allowed only on book monthly. There are no due dates for either service, but you must swap books within the unlimited subscription to maintain only ten monthly. The lending library has no audiobook availability, kindle unlimited has over 65, 00 available. The kindle unlimited subscription is accessible from kindle applications, and the lending library is not. Both services have many titles to choose from, passing the 1,000,000 mark.

Kindle lending library and kindle unlimited subscription have thirty-day free trial periods so that you can test it out before you make a commitment to a monthly payment.

The lists of eligible books for both services are very similar. With over one million titles to choose from, many are exclusive only to kindle services. Out of approximately one million books, only 40, 00 are not considered exclusive. Big publishing companies are not affiliated with kindle lending library or with kindle unlimited subscription. You may see this as a weak point, or not. Most books are very affordable if you do decide that you want to own them permanently. That has to do with the fact that these services are not involved with big publishing houses. Despite the absence of the big publishing houses, there are many titles available.

There are benefits to both these services, and the differences are so slight that they are barely noticeable. But, like all good customers, spending money wisely is important. From a consumer's perspective, the biggest plus to kindle lending library is the variety of media services. The biggest plus in kindle unlimited is the wide variety of books in prevalent categories. Also, kindle unlimited has audiobooks. With plenty of new authors to choose from, kindle unlimited shows its merits through variability.

Discovering new books is always an incredible part of a reader's literacy experience. Kindle unlimited subscription, although similar to kindle lending library, shines through with its uniqueness.

Chapter7: *Signing Up*

Mostly based on reputation, the kindle unlimited subscription is the best eBook subscription for your money. Everyone wants to get the most out of everything that they choose to invest in. This subscription not only includes the remarkable range of eBooks, but also the audio books. The audiobook are individual titles, as well as companion titles.

The kindle unlimited subscription is ideal for people that read a lot. Kindle unlimited subscription gives everyone a free thirty day trail period, and allows you to select audio books as well during that time.

This provides you with an opportunity to really experience using the subscription. It also gives you a chance to look over the lists of books and authors that are available at the time. The titles are ever changing, so you can gauge what you commit to and what you do not commit to. This type of tractability is hard to find with many other eBook reading services. Thirty days is a sufficient amount of time to make an educated decision. Whether or not you would like to fully commit to the unlimited subscription, you still can get a pretty good idea of what it entails for future reference.

At such a cost effective price, it would be almost a waste not to take full advantage of the unlimited subscription. When you compare it to other eBook services, you will quickly see the full advantages. Even before you become a subscriber, you can fully explore all the wonderful and interesting titles kindle's unlimited subscription has to offer. Once you have begun to understand better more how it all works, you will discover how easy it is. You just enter with your account and subscribe. Then, you open yourself up to a whole new world of reading pleasure.

The flexibility to choose and then return used eBooks is not a new concept. Yet, while using the kindle unlimited subscription, you would believe that it is. Its range of compatibility with other devices ensures that you never lose your place in the book that you're reading. In this technologically influenced day and age, having many devices is not uncommon. Having your office or home at your fingertips has become a common passing. This experience is enhanced by the world of applications. Applications are mini-programs that allow you download games, music, photos, and a variety of other add-ons to your devices.

So, how do you sign up? It's actually a very simple process. The first step is you need to sign into Amazon.com. with your account.

Click on the Kindle Unlimited page. There you can sign up for you thirty-day free trial. Also, includes is a three-month trial to the audio books selection. Now you can start exploring the possibilities of kindle unlimited. If you choose to keep it after thirty days, simply continue using it. If you aren't ready to commit at the moment, after your thirty-day trial, just go back to the amazon web page and cancel your subscription. It really is as easy as that. Remember, once you stop payment on your subscription, the books that you have on your devices will no longer be available.

Here is a list of some of the most recent titles you can currently enjoy with your kindle unlimited subscription. They all have a five-star rating or above:

- Peony by Pearl S. Buck
- White Spirit (A novel based on a true story) by Lance Morgan
- Forbid Me (The Good Ol' Boys #2) By M. Robinson
- Atlantis On The Shores of Forever (Atlantis #1) by Jennifer Mckeithen
- Sky Diamond by Anna Brockton
- Finding Stone (Stone Brothers #1) by T. Saint John
- The Dinosaur Four by Geoff Jones
- The Button by Nicholas Ponticello
- Creating Monsters by Christopher Rankin
- Tagged: The Apocalypse by Joseph M. Chiron

- Love you to Death: A Psychological Crime Thriller by Rita Ames
- Killing Katie by Brain Spangler
- Lord Fish by Ted Cross
- Maude by Donna Mabry
- Chasing Payne by Chantel Seabrook
- Wreckage by Emily Bleeker
- Alpha by A.D. Rawat
- Under the Volcano by Malcolm Lowry
- How to train your Knight: A Medieval Romance by Stella Marie Alden
- Cara's Twelve by Chantel Seabrook
- The Birthday Card by Sandra Foley
- Fishing in Potato Salad by Othen Donald dale Cummings
- Dreams Come True by Bridgitte Lesley
- The Handmaid's Tale by Margaret Atwood
- Use Somebody by Riley Jean
- Luck of the Irish: Complete Edition
- Life of Pi by Yann Martel
- Forever Torn by Jason Greenfield
- The Unseen Man by Jason Greenfield
- Caligatha by Matt spice
- The Heart is a Lonely Hunter by Carson McCullers
- Up the Down Staircase by Bel Kaufman

- The Princess Bride by William Goldman
- Wonder Boys by Michael Chabon
- The Namesake by Jhumpa Lahiri
- Extremely Loud and Incredibly Close by Jonathan Safran Foer
- Pocket Kings by Ted Heller
- The Art Forger: A Novel by B.A. Shapiro
- The Night Gwen Stacy Died by Sarah Bruni
- Want Not by Johnathan Miles
- The Man Who Mistook His wife For a Hat and Other Clinical Tales by Oliver Sacks
- The New World by Winston Churchill
- The Theory of Relativity and Other Essays by Albert Einstein
- Oh, Myyy! By George Takei
- More Than Scars by Sarah Brocious
- Followed by Frost by Charlie N. Holmberg
- Thorn by Intisar Khanani
- The Grand Sophy by Georgette Heyer
- Princess Ahira by K.M.Shea
- Cotillion by Georgette Heyer

Conclusion

Having a kindle is a great way to stay in constant contact with the joy of reading. Throughout the years, the kindle in companion with Amazon has enriched reader's lives, all around the world. Kindles and kindle related services are in over one hundred and eighty countries. Providing amazing and reliable services to enhance the kindle experience is another way kindle continually shows the commitment they have to the reader. The affordability and easy management system all allow for a better overall experience.

The portability of the kindle has made it an obvious choice for travelers. Now, with kindle unlimited subscription, your subscription goes where you go, on any device.

The wide selection of classics and modern hits ensures that there is something for every reader. It is outright useful to have ease of access to books at all times, on all your devices.

A great alternative to buying books nowadays, the kindle unlimited subscription eliminates the purchase worry that you may not be getting what you have already paid for. The month-long switching period is ample enough time to consider if the eBook you have chosen will soon become a lasting part of your library.

It's the most fantastic book swap without the hassle of lugging books around with you! It is discreet in the fact that you can be on your device, and it won't seem unfriendly, because, after all, you're reading a book. Using your kindle unlimited subscription blurs the line between traditional library customs and technological norms that are ever present now. The excitement of divulging into a whole new genus of reading materials can only be pleasing to the knowledgeable book fanatic.

The vast inventory of kindle unlimited subscription books is made up of many independent authors. This is important to think about in the big picture. By not subsuming to the big publishing cooperation, you are helping new authors perhaps publish their very next book. Everyone enjoys helping out the little guy, especially if it is through something we love.

People are basically sharing their stories and you get to enjoy them all. The other great thing is that you can also hear all your stories, because of the wonderful audiobooks available. Most of the all-time classics are available as audiobooks. Imagine on your next road trip listening to Dickens or Miguel de Cervantes. That would definitely make your time on the road much more enjoyable. With so many titles to choose from, you may begin taking more road trips just to listen to your favorites.

The kindle unlimited subscription is the easiest and fastest way to open up you reading library. Sharing your love of literature with others by recommending the new authors you find. Being able to budget in your passion for reading every month is not only amazing, it is a privilege. Finding all the books you want is a piece of cake, anywhere, at any time.

Browsing is made easy with the unlimited website, and searching for your new books is made fun. Having thousands of novels instantly at your fingertips changes you're construing literary experience in so many ways. Intelligent people thirst for new knowledge, and the best place to find it is in books. Interchanging books that you can eventually own is like having your own private book club, that you completely control and master. We use books as solace, comfort, and adventure. We have so much invested in our reading time, that we should defiantly do everything in our power to make it sacred and important. We can do this by being consistently exposed to new and fresh ideas through literacy.

Accepting the advances of eBooks and all the treasures they hold, we as readers will discover what it really means to be a reader in this day and age. What it really means to conserve our planet by using less paper. What it really means to exploit technology to its full advantage. With your kindle unlimited subscription, not even the sky is the limit, because the subscription is out of this world.

www.ingramcontent.com/pod-product-compliance
Lightning Source LLC
Chambersburg PA
CBHW070906070326
40690CB00009B/2025